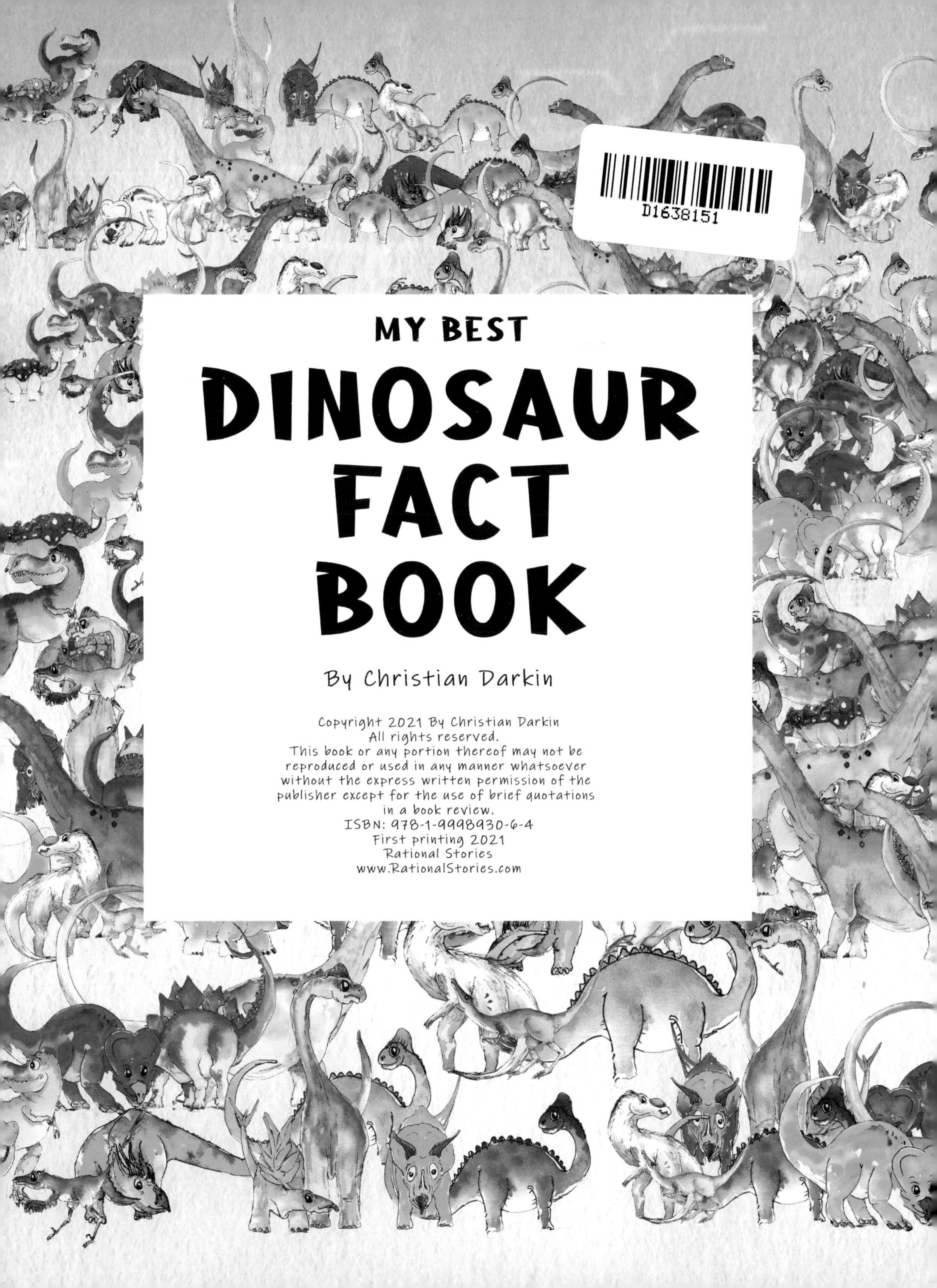

MY BEST

DINOSAUR FACT BOOK

By Christian Darkin

ISBN: 978-1-9998930-6-4
First printing 2021
Rational Stories
www.RationalStories.com

DINOSAURS LIVED ALL OVER THE WORLD.

SOME DINOSAURS LIVED
IN THE DESERT.

SOME DINOSAURS LIVED
IN THE SNOW.

SWIMMING REPTILES WERE NOT DINOSAURS...

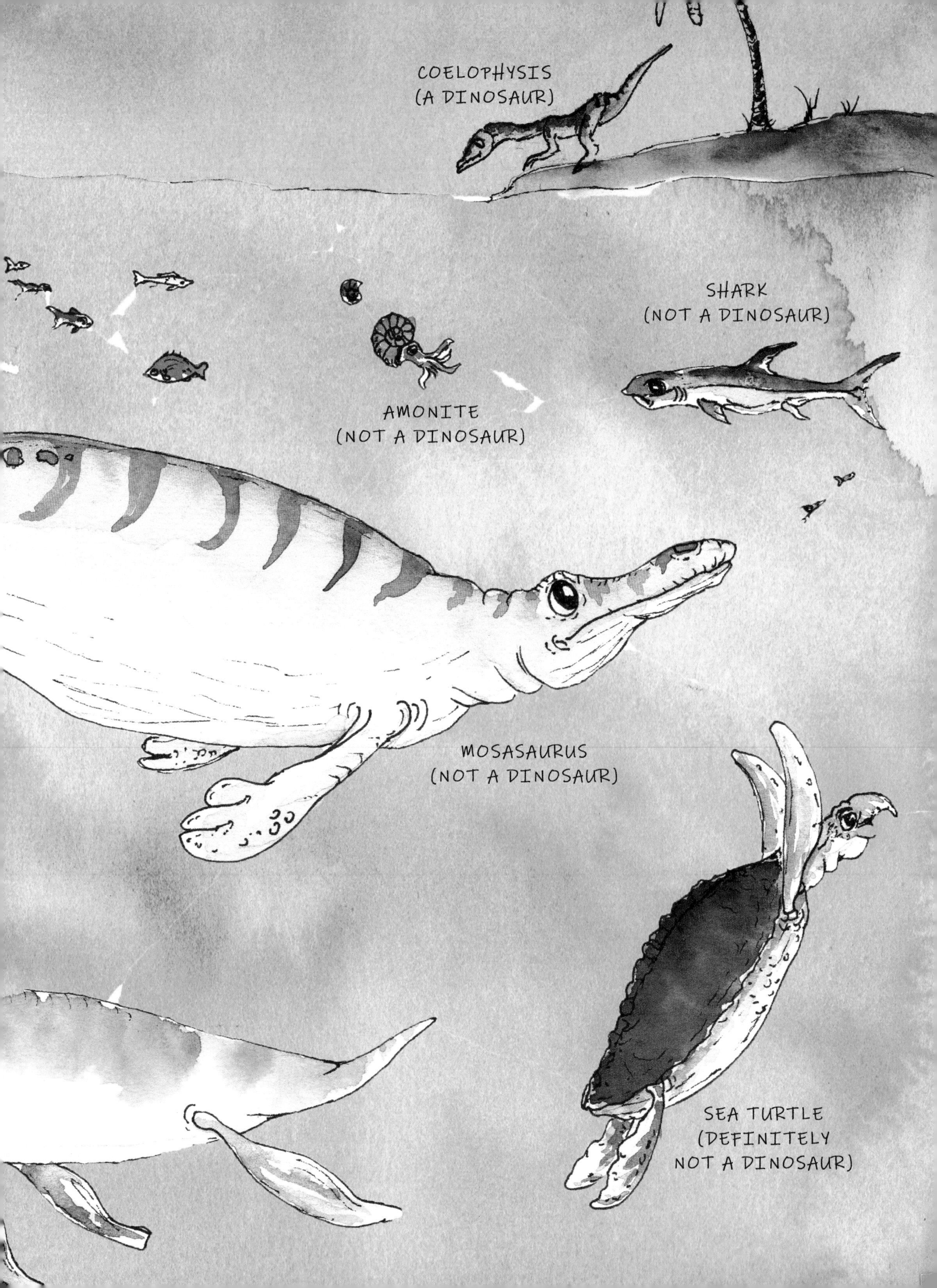
COELOPHYSIS
(A DINOSAUR)
SHARK
(NOT A DINOSAUR)
AMONITE
(NOT A DINOSAUR)
MOSASAURUS
(NOT A DINOSAUR)
SEA TURTLE
(DEFINITELY
NOT A DINOSAUR)

...NEITHER WERE FLYING REPTILES...

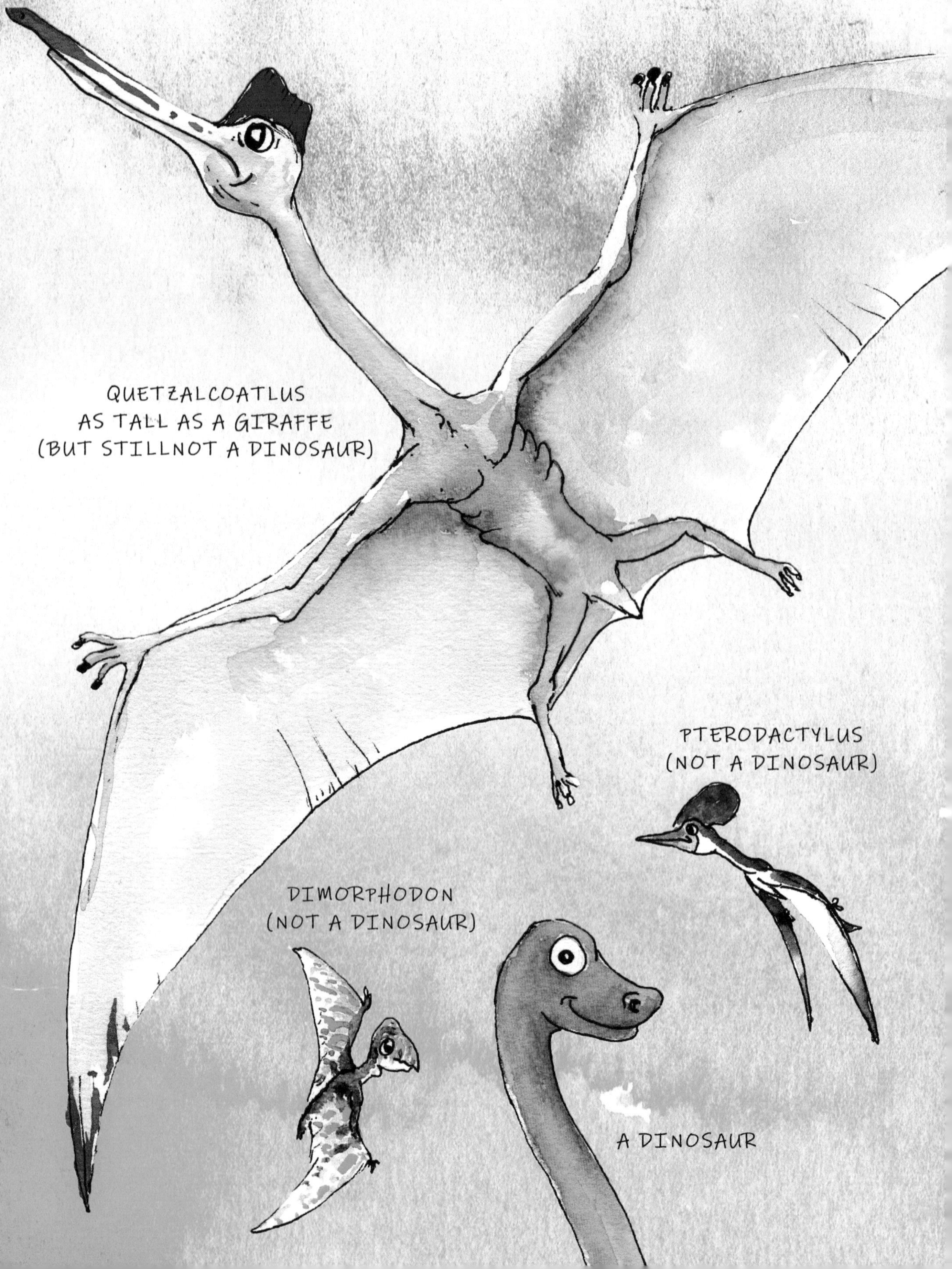

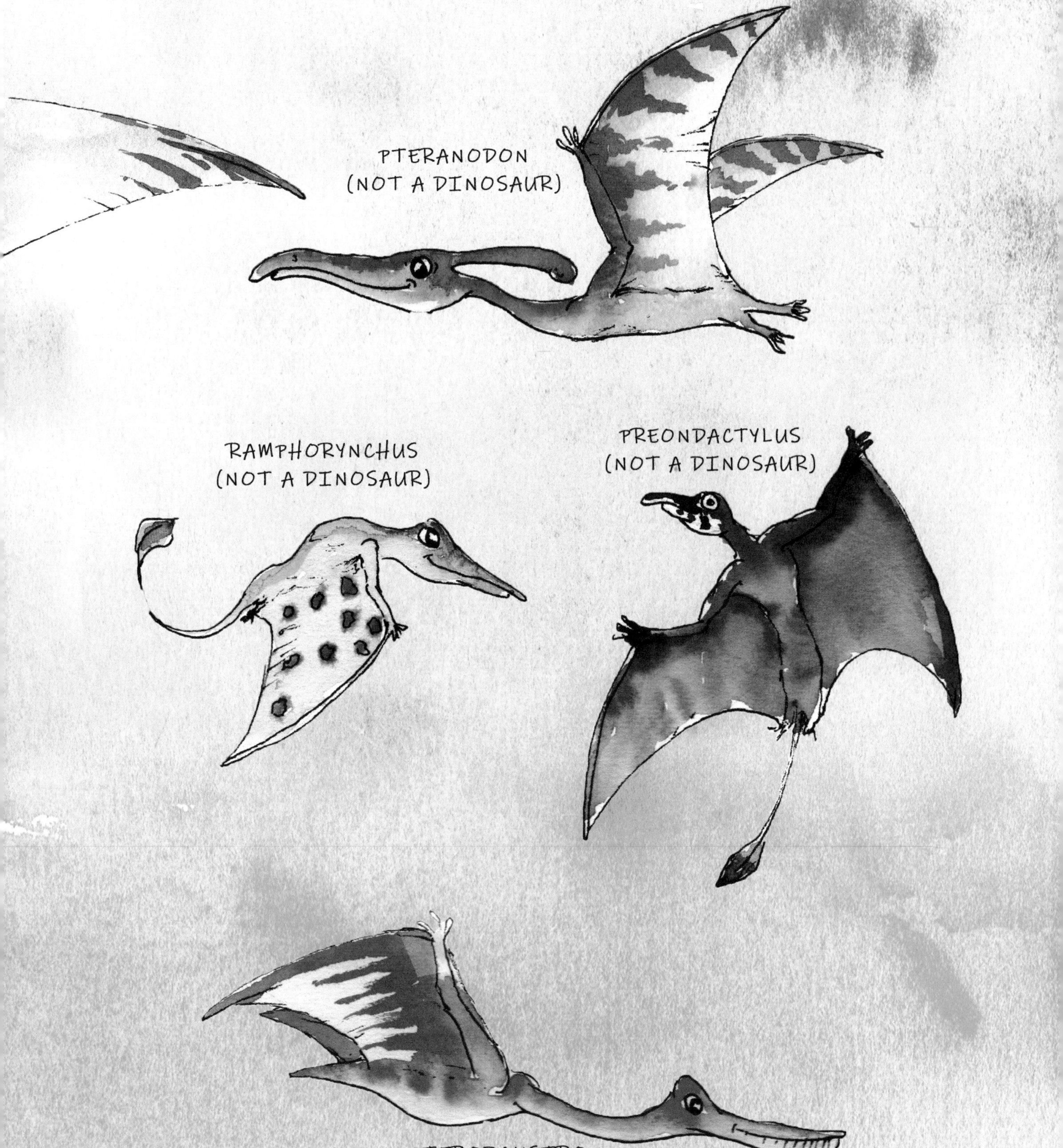
PTERANODON
(NOT A DINOSAUR)
RAMPHORYNCHUS
(NOT A DINOSAUR)
PREONDACTYLUS
(NOT A DINOSAUR)
PTERODAUSTRO
(NOT A DINOSAUR)

...BUT ALL BIRDS ARE DINOSAURS.

LOTS OF DINOSAURS HAD BEAKS...

...AND LOTS HAD FEATHERS TOO.

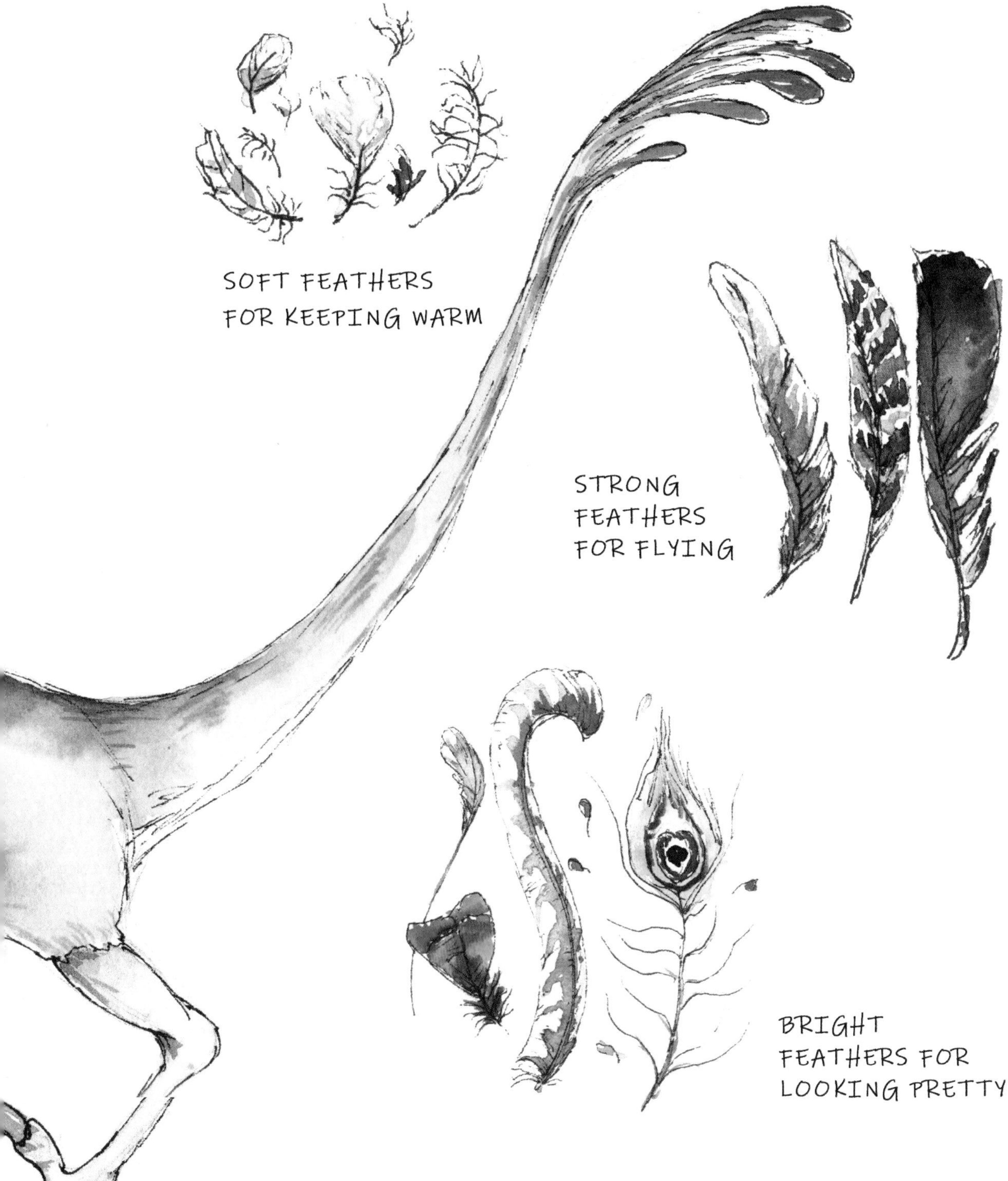

SOFT FEATHERS
FOR KEEPING WARM

STRONG
FEATHERS
FOR FLYING

BRIGHT
FEATHERS FOR
LOOKING PRETTY

WHAT SORT OF FEATHERS CAN
YOU FIND?

TYRANNOSAURUS REX HAD A LOT OF COUSINS...

...BUT WE DON'T KNOW WHAT COLOURS THEY WERE.

CAN YOU COLOUR THEM?

BARYONYX

CARNOTAURUS

SPINOSAURUS

COELOPHYSIS

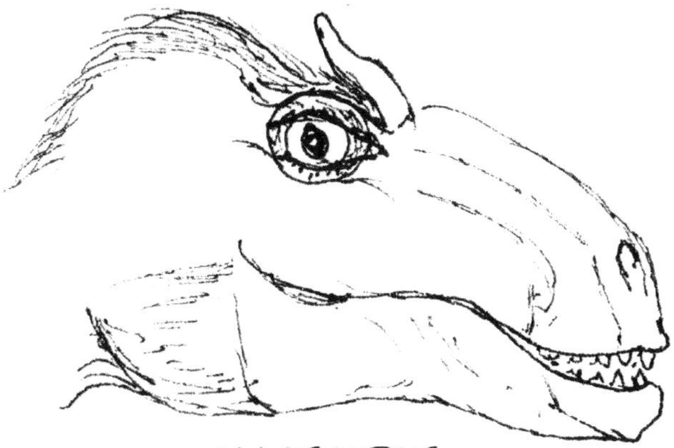

ALLOSAURUS

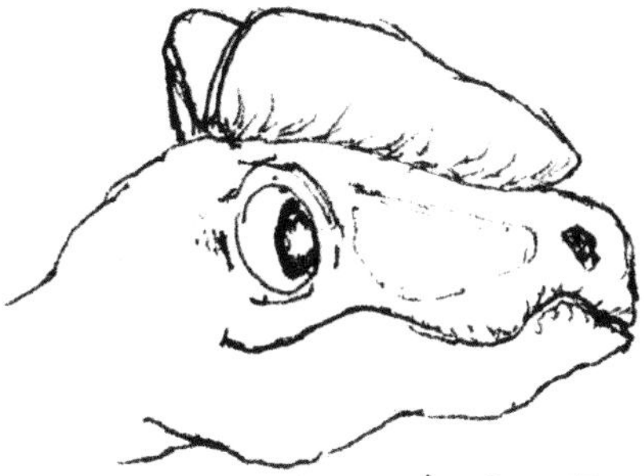

DILOPHOSAURUS

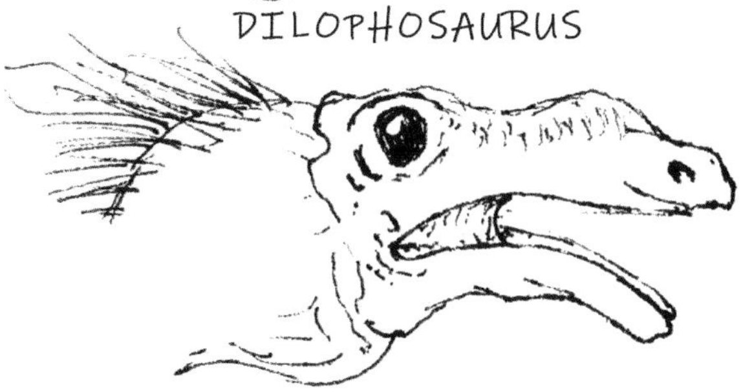

THERIZINOSAURUS

CHICKEN

TRICERATOPS HAD LOTS OF COUSINS TOO...

DIABLOCERATOPS

STYRACOSAURUS

PROTOCERATOPS

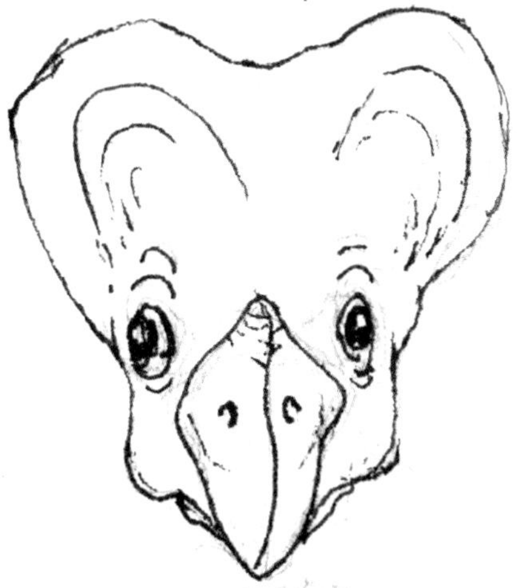

TRICERATOPS

KOSMOCERATOPS

WHATEVER-YOU-WANT-
ACERATOPS

...AND SO DID STEGOSAURUS.

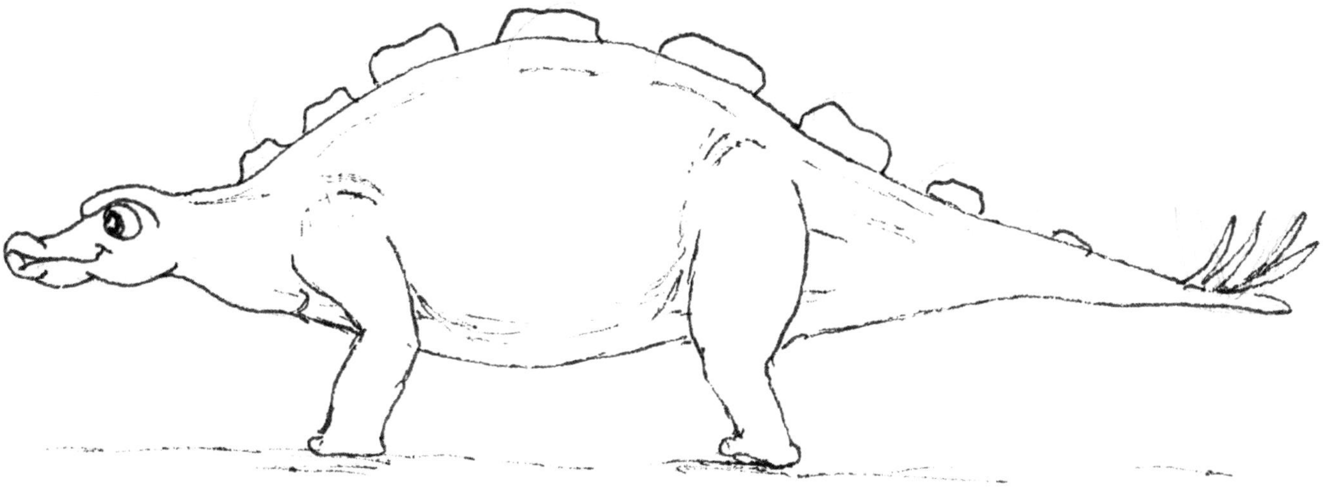

WUERHOSAURUS

HUAYANGOSAURUS

KENTROSAURUS

TUOJIANGOSAURUS

ARGENTINOSAURUS WAS THE BIGGEST DINOSAUR FOUND SO FAR.

YOUR HOUSE AFTER ARGENTINOSAURUS HAS GONE PAST.

YOUR HOUSE BEFORE
ARGENTINOSAURUS
GOES PAST.

SOME DINOSAURS WERE VERY SMALL.

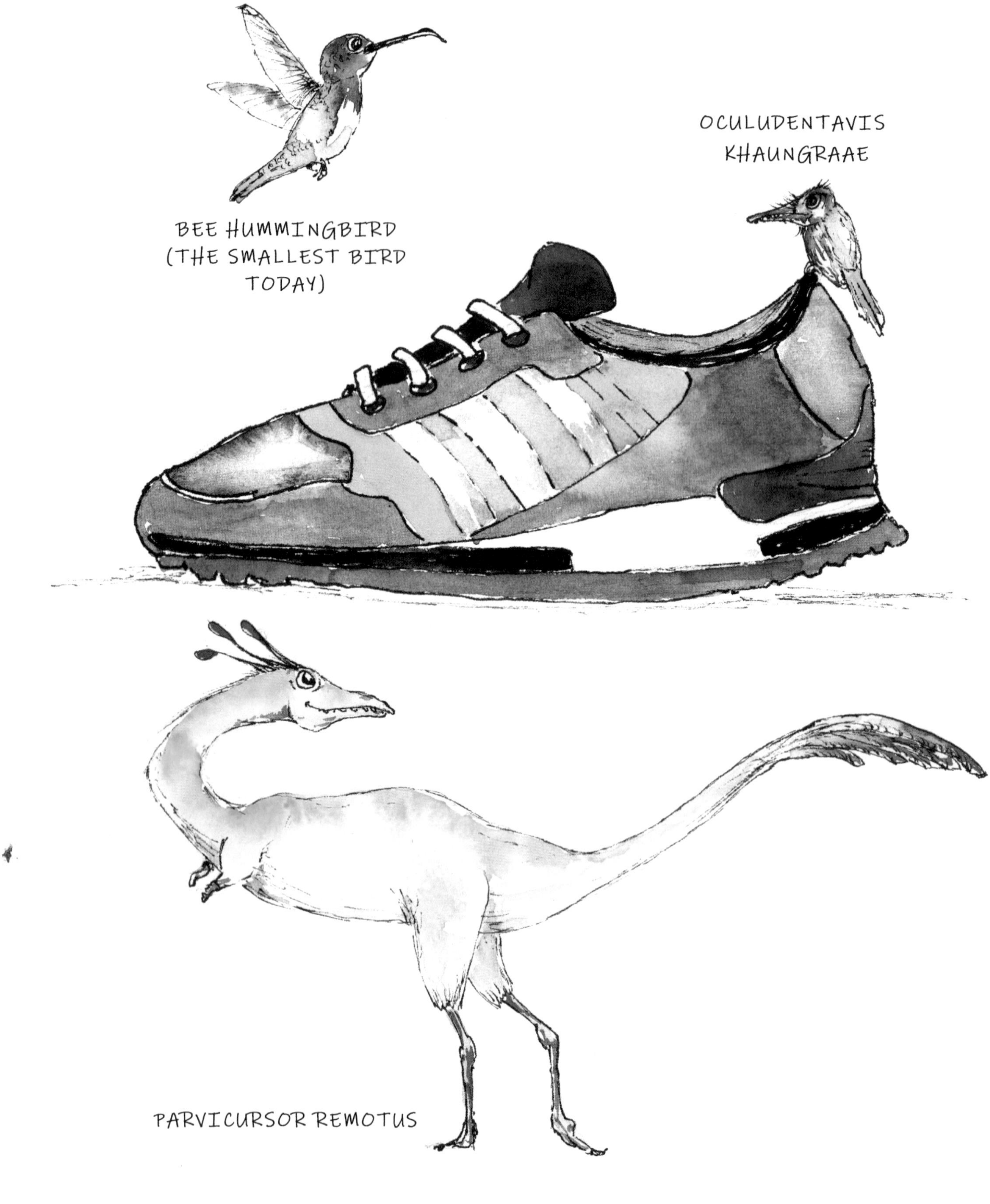

STEGOSAURUS WAS AS BIG AS A BUS

BUT ITS BRAIN WAS THE SIZE OF A WALNUT.

700 DIFFERENT TYPES OF DINOSAUR HAVE BEEN FOUND SO FAR.

HOW MANY OF EACH KIND CAN YOU SEE HERE?

MOST DINOSAURS WITH
FOUR LEGS ATE PLANTS.

MOST DINOSAURS WITH TWO LEGS DIDN'T.

WE KNOW WHAT DINOSAURS ATE
MOSTLY FROM THEIR POO

WHAT DO YOU THINK
THESE DINOSAURS ATE?

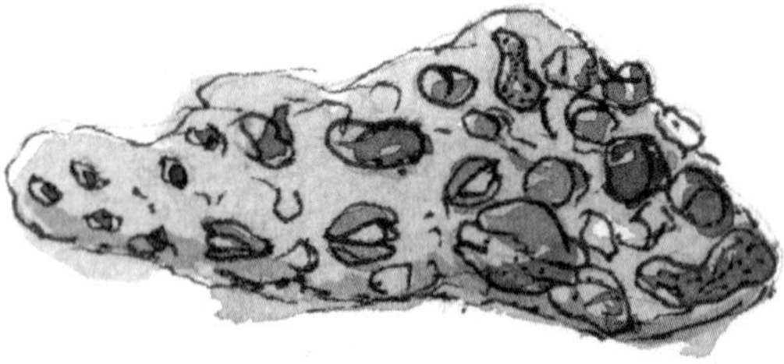

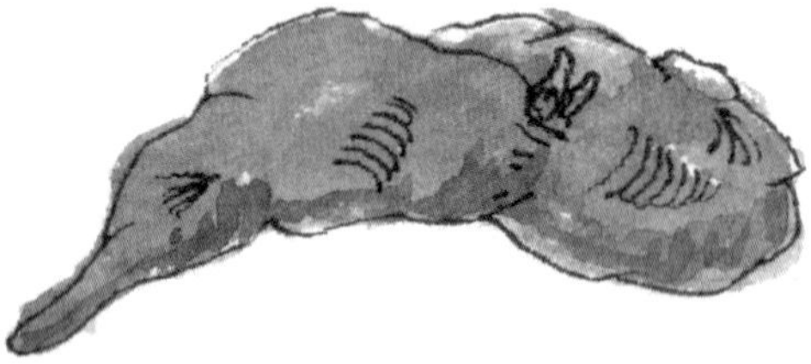

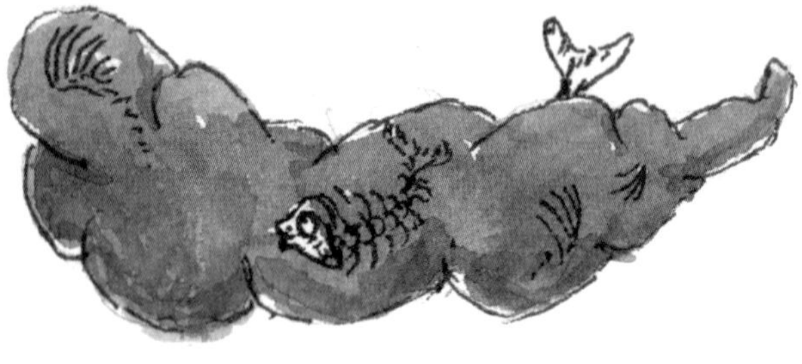

AND FROM THEIR TEETH.

POINTY TEETH
FOR EATING MEAT

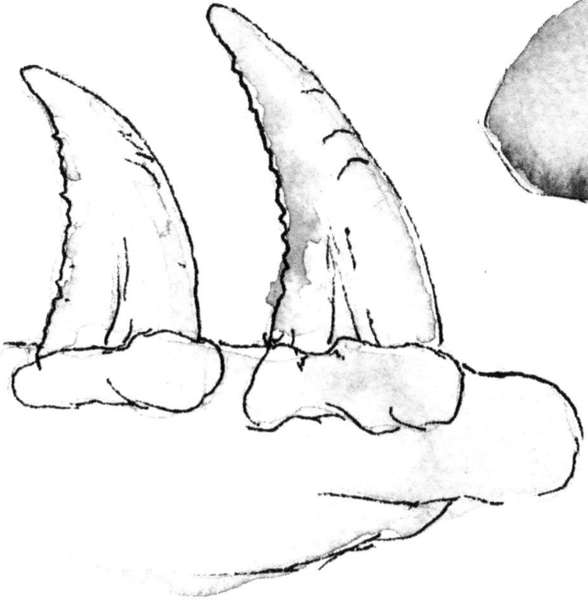

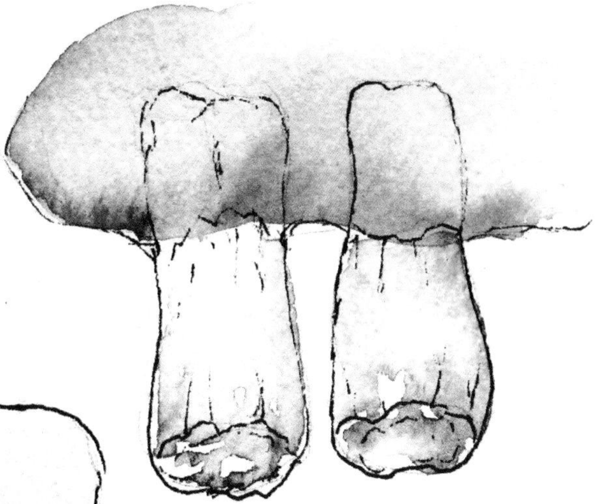

FLAT TEETH FOR PLANTS

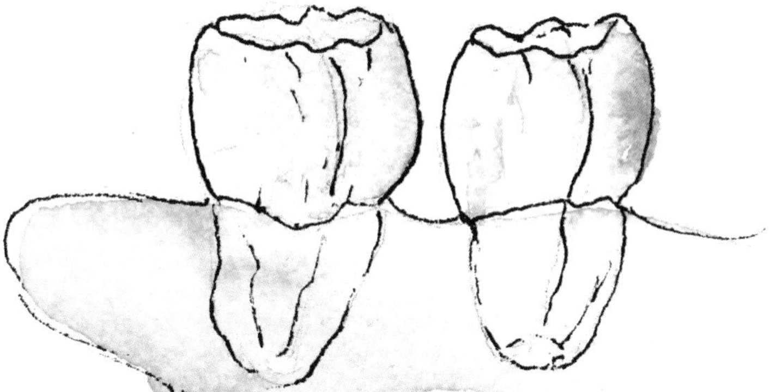

SPIKY TEETH FOR
SLIPPERY FISH

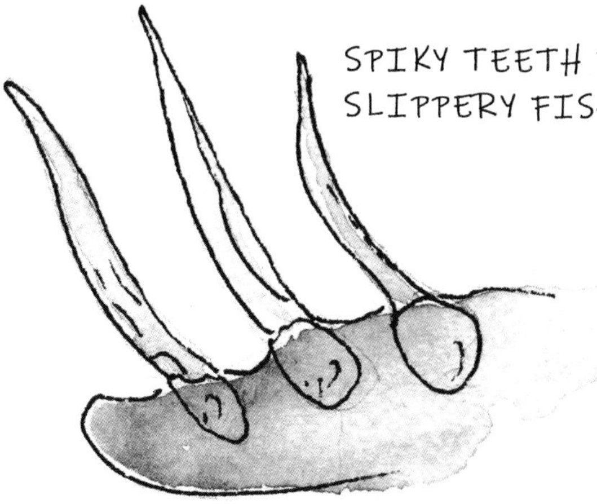

THIS IS HOW LIFE STARTED...

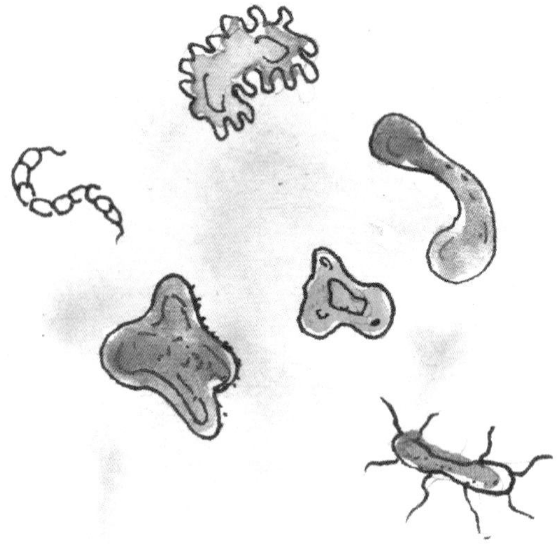

FOR A LONG TIME
THERE WERE JUST TINY BLOBS
IN THE SEA.

THEN SOME OF THE BLOBS
GOT TAILS AND HEADS AND BECAME
WORMS AND FISHES.

MUCH LATER,
SOME OF THE FISHES
GREW LEGS AND
BECAME LIZARDS.

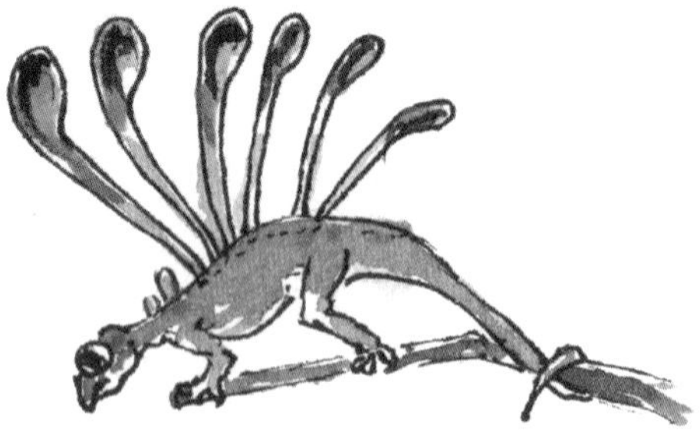

THEN CAME
THE DINOSAURS...

LOTS OF
DINOSAURS...

THEN, AFTER THE BIG
DINOSAURS HAD GONE,
CAME THE MAMMALS,
AND PEOPLE.

ALL THE BIG DINOSAURS
ARE GONE NOW.

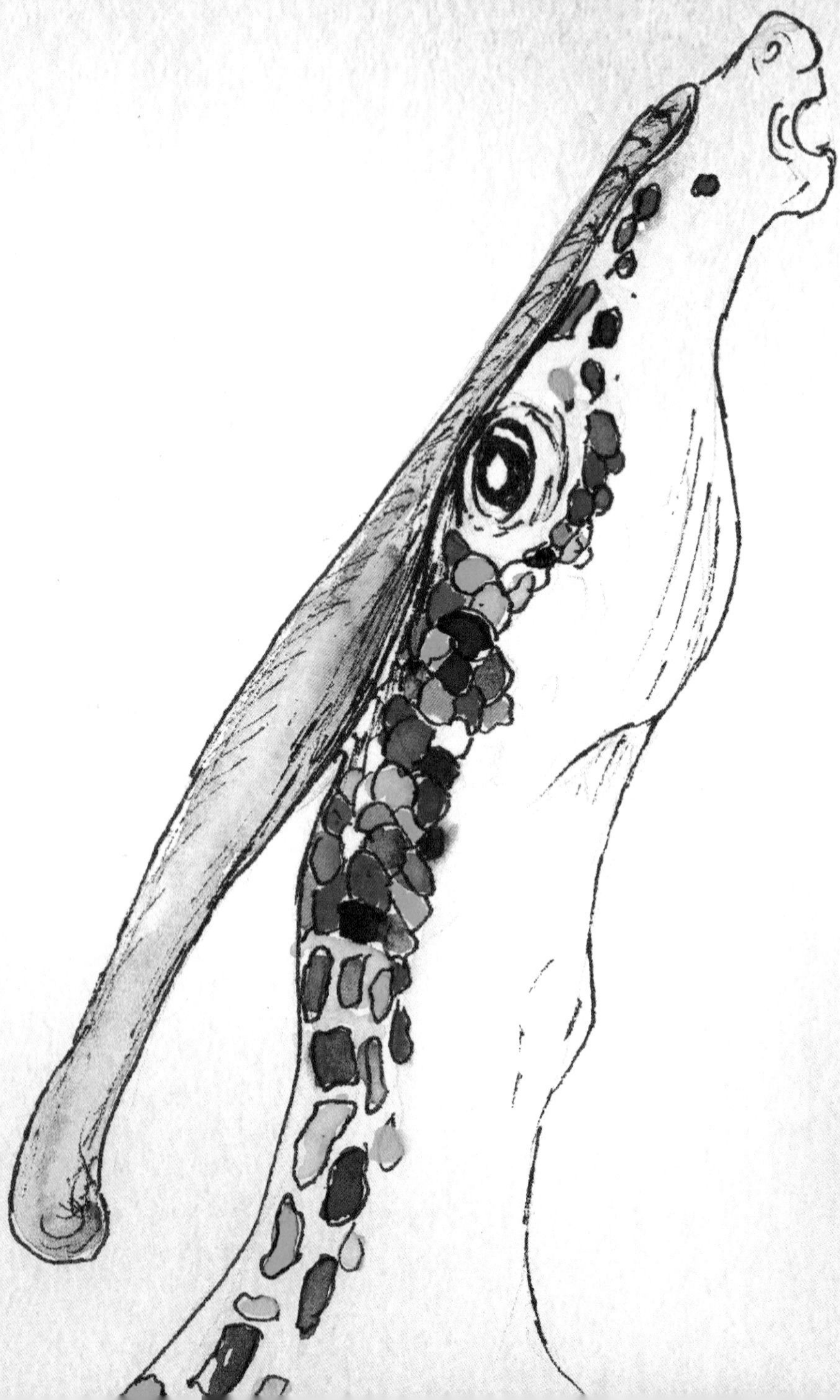

ONLY THE BIRDS ARE LEFT.
HOW MANY DINOSAURS HAVE YOU SEEN TODAY?

WE KNOW ABOUT DINOSAURS
BECAUSE WE FIND THEIR BONES.

HOW MANY DINOSAUR SKULLS CAN YOU COUNT?

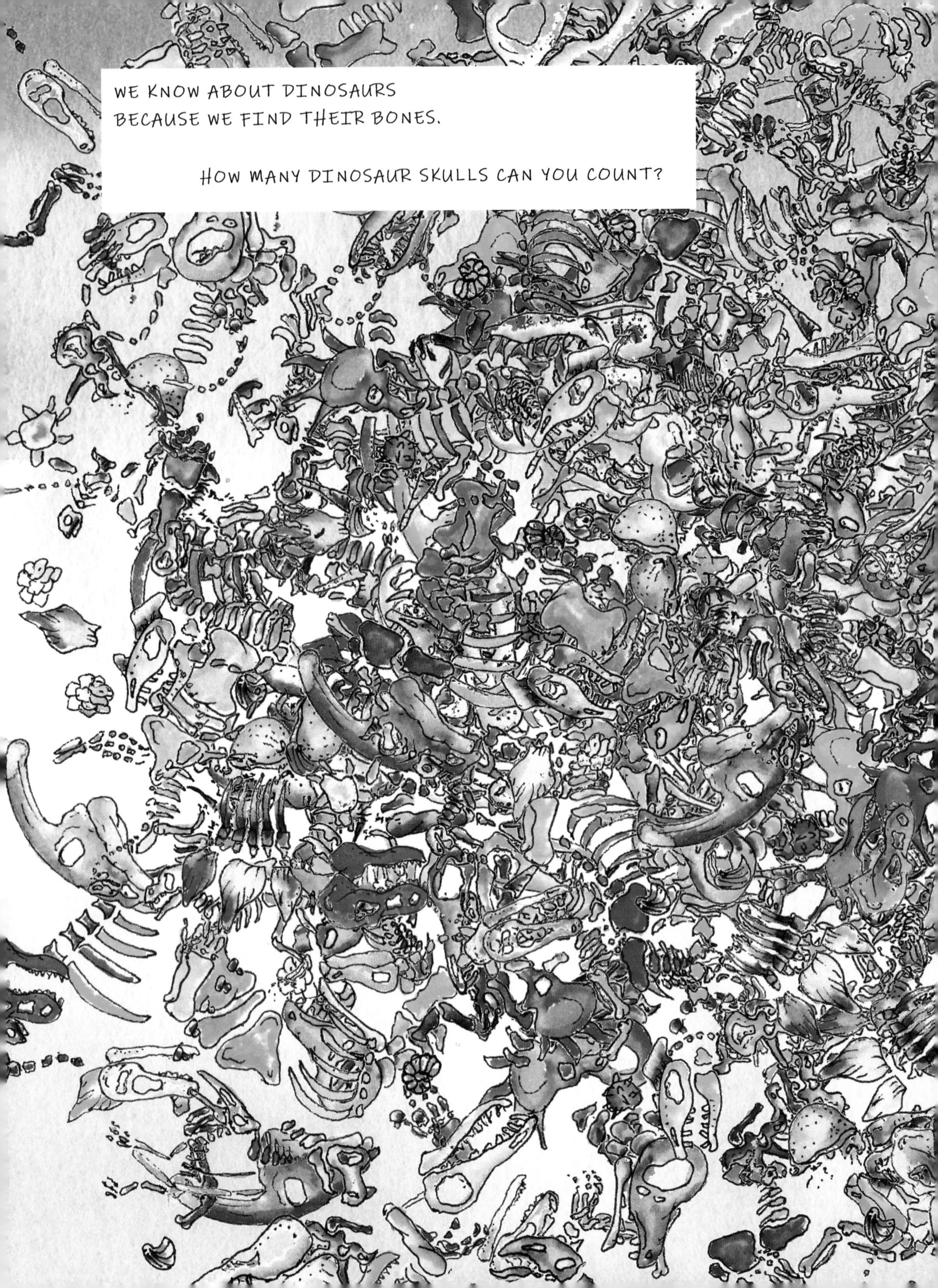

I really hope you enjoyed this book.

If you did, please take a moment to put a review on Amazon, mention it on social media, or just tell a friend. It really helps to spread the word.

Thanks so much,
Christian Darkin
Author/Illustrator

You can also email me directly at
christian@anachronistic.co.uk
Or tweet @animateddad
I'd love to hear from you.